RHS GROW YOUR OWN *for kids*

RHS GROW YOUR OWN
for kids

The Blue Peter Gardener Chris Collins
and Lia Leendertz

mitchell Beazley

An Hachette UK Company
www.hachette.co.uk

First published in Great Britain in 2012 by
MItchell Beazley, a division of Octopus Publishing Group Ltd
Endeavour House,
189 Shaftesbury Avenue
London
WC2H 8JY
www.octopusbooks.co.uk

Copyright © Octopus Publishing Group Ltd 2012
Published in association with the Royal Horticultural Society

ISBN 978 1 84533 510 6

A CIP catalogue record for this book is available from the
British Library

Printed and bound in China

10 9 8 7 6 5 4 3 2 1

For the RHS:
Publisher: Rae Spencer-Jones
Consultant editor: Simon Maughan

For Octopus Publishing Group:
Publishers: Lorraine Dickey & Alison Starling
Editorial Director: Tracey Smith
Senior Production Controller: Lucy Carter
Art Direction and Design: Tracy Killick
Editorial management: Helen Griffin
Editor: Caroline Taggart, Alex Stetter
Photography: Will Heap

Here's what's inside

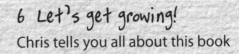

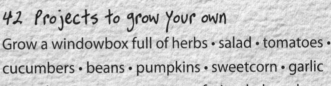

Let's get growing!

On a sunny spring morning, I cannot wait to get outside and check the seedlings that I planted a few days before. It's so exciting! Whether you plant one special sunflower or a whole plot of vegetables, seeing things grow is one of the real wonders of life.

What if I haven't got a garden?

You don't need masses of space or even a garden to be a great gardener – a window-box can give you fresh herbs for pizzas, pasta, salads and sandwiches. Why not try growing a strawberry fountain or use a hanging basket to grow tomatoes? They are great fun to grow and things you pick from your own plants are going to be fresher and far more tasty than anything you can buy in the shops. There is nothing like it. Remember though, give your plants a little bit of your time every day – don't forget to feed, water and give your plants lots of love.

Be a wildlife warrior

When you dig a piece of ground or turn over the soil to take out weeds and stones, it's great fun to watch how many birds you attract to your veg plot. Bees, butterflies, and other helpful insects can be encouraged to visit your garden by planting certain flowers. In turn, these insects will help your plants to grow by spreading pollen and seeds and eating pests. If you work with wildlife, they will do a lot of the work for you.

Green gardening is great

Nature is very clever but it also needs your help and you can be a green gardener by saving water as you garden. Try to put as much water back into your soil as your plants take out of it. Making compost is fun and if you don't have room for a compost heap, perhaps you can build one at school or in a friend's garden. Then lots of you can save things from your plants and your kitchen to put onto it. You can even make home-made fertiliser for your plants by keeping worms – this book will show you how!

So now you're a gardener

As you pick your first fruit and veg, you will see what fun it is to grow things. Everyone loves to be given great things to eat, but don't forget that you can give away some of your baby plants as well – in that way even more people can have fun gardening. Being a gardener will keep you and your friends busy, happy and well fed and there's no better way to enjoy the great world outdoors.

So, welcome to the wonderful world of gardening!

Chris

You can start small —why not sow some seeeds in a box for your window sill?

Gardening with other people is even more fun than gardening on your own!

You're going to be a great gardener!

setting up a vegetable garden

If you have a garden, your vegetables will do a lot of the work for you, as their roots will search for food and water in the earth. So the first thing for you to do is to learn about your soil.

Where should your garden be?

You may not be able to decide exactly where your vegetable garden will be, but if you can choose, remember a few things. Most vegetables love the sun so pick the sunniest spot you can. Plants don't like wind so try to to make sure your plot is sheltered. You will need to give your plants lots of water so try to pick a spot near to an outdoor tap or not too far from your home. And one last thing, the roots of large plants and trees use up lots of the goodness in the soil, so keep your veg patch away from them if you can.

What's your soil like?

Squeeze a handful of soil in your hand. If it feels smooth and squelchy, it is probably clay soil. If it feels crumbly and grainy, it is sandy soil. The best soil is not too squelchy and not too grainy, but don't panic if yours is not! You can make any soil better by adding well-rotted compost or manure. Try and grow things that suit your soil type, for example, lots of herbs like sandy soils, and fruit trees prefer growing in clay.

squelchy soil is probably clay soil but crumbly soil is likely to be sandy soil

How big is YOUR bed?

Where you plant your vegetables is called a bed. Make sure that yours is small enough for you to reach into the middle without trampling all over the soil. If your bed is bigger than that, you will need to leave a path in the middle. Make sure your path is wide enough to push a wheelbarrow along.

the science

CHRIS EXPLAINS:
SOIL
Soil is different in one garden from the next, and each soil type is good and bad in different ways. Clay soil is dense, which makes it good at hanging on to nutrients (the food plants need), but it is hard to dig. Sandy soil is very loose, so roots can grow easily, and water drains away quickly. But it loses nutrients quickly and can dry out easily, which means you have to add lots of compost.

Walk along your patch, gently pressing down the soil with your feet

Getting your patch ready

Before you plant anything, you need to make your patch as perfect as possible. First you need to dig your patch to remove weeds and add air, and to help the soil to absorb water. When you have done this, use a rake to get rid of any big stones that have been uncovered by your digging. Finally, walk up and down your plot, pressing the soil back down gently, being careful on tread on every bit of soil.

Gorgeous garden waste

Saving garden waste and turning it into compost to spread over your beds really helps to keep the soil in great condition. But be careful that you use the right ingredients to make it!

Compost is great and, by making it yourself, it is also free!

Piling up the goodness

Great compost needs the right ingredients and plenty of air. If you don't have both of these, it will be slimy and smelly. Use a mixture of things that rot quickly (like grass clippings and even food from your kitchen) and things that will take longer to rot but will help to keep plenty of air in your compost heap (like straw, twigs, or cardboard).

Designing your compost bin

You *can* just throw your compost ingredients into a pile, but a compost bin is neater and works better. Storing compost in a bin helps to build up heat in the heap, which makes it rot down more quickly. Home-made bins made from slatted wood let air into the heap and are great (make sure it has a door in the front so you can get to your compost), but you can buy plastic ones that work well too.

Cover your heap to heat it up and it will make compost more quickly

Turning the heap

To make compost quickly, you must turn your compost over after a few months. This will help to get air right into the middle of the heap, which keeps the temperature up. To do this, first take away the bin, or the front of it, dig out all the compost, put the bin back and then put all the compost back in it. Phew.

In the heap or out? Friend or enemy?

IN	OUT
Leaf trimmings	Cooked food
Grass clippings	Fruit
Raw veg peelings	Eggs
Thin twigs and straw	Meat
Newspaper	Thick tree prunings
Cardboard	Plastic

Spreading the goodness

Once you've made your compost and it's ready to use, you need to spread it around the garden where needed. Use a bucket to take it to your beds from the compost heap and then use a fork to mix it into the earth. This will help your soil to stay in tiptop condition – it's a bit like giving it a huge dose of vitamins!

Home-made compost is health food for your garden

How high is your bed?

If your soil isn't good enough or you want to have a small patch to call your own, you could make a raised bed and fill it with multi-purpose potting compost, which you can buy in garden centres.

Working in the garden with your friends is fun

1 BEFORE YOU CAN START TO USE YOUR RAISED BED, cover the base in thick cardboard. This will kill any grass and weeds underneath it. Then fill the bed with compost. Rake the compost carefully to get rid of any stones or lumps.

2 NOW TREAD DOWN THE SOIL TO GET RID OF ANY POCKETS OF AIR. It's more fun to do this with your friends. Now try to be patient – it's best to let the contents settle for a week or two. You may then need to top up the compost.

To make a raised bed, you need help from an adult who is good at DIY

3 TO HELP YOU TO PLANT IN STRAIGHT LINES use a string tied to two sticks. Put one stick at each end of the line you want to mark and push the sticks into the compost, pulling the string tight as you do so.

Building a raised bed

If you don't have a special kit, perhaps an adult will agree to make a raised bed for you. To do this, mark out the sides of the bed, then use a spade to clear away any turf from where the raised bed's walls are going to lie. A spirit level will help to get the area roughly flat. Lay four planks on the ground. Drill holes through the ends and use long, heavy-duty coach screws to fix the joints together as shown. A corner brace will add strength. Make the beds the depth of a single plank, or stack several 'frames' on top of one another and fix them together to make something deeper.

4 IT'S EASY TO LOOK AFTER YOUR PLANTS IN A RAISED BED because you won't have to walk on top of your newly planted seedlings and you can just reach into the middle of the bed without bending too far.

Tubs, pots and containers

Don't worry if you don't have a vegetable patch. Lots of plants will grow really well in pots or other containers on balconies or windowsills. Perhaps your school will have room for some too.

Choosing your pot

Always pick a big pot. Small amounts of compost dry out quickly, so plants in small pots will need more attention than those in larger ones. But you must be careful not to let the soil in any container dry out.

Letting the water out

Roots will rot if the soil in a container is too damp. Check that your pots have a hole in the bottom to let water out. (If they don't, ask an adult to make some for you.) Put broken pieces of old pots over the holes to stop the water from washing away the compost.

What to plant in?

Any good quality, multi-purpose potting compost is ideal, which is available at any garden centre or even in some large supermarkets.

Use your fingers to break up any big lumps in your compost

Use bits of broken plant pots — or even small stones — to help water to drain away from your pots

16

the science

CHRIS EXPLAINS: PLANTING IN POTS

Plants growing in pots (rather than in the ground) need a bit more attention and care. Make sure the compost is firm when you do your planting and press out all of the air pockets. This allows water to travel through the soil easily and be taken up by the plants' roots. Always leave a gap at the top of the pot for watering – if you don't, the water will overflow and wash the compost from the pot.

Plants to eat that grow well in pots

Tomatoes	Strawberries
Chillis	Citrus trees
Sweet peppers	Herbs
Aubergines	Dwarf French beans
Carrots	Courgettes
Lettuce	Blueberries
Spring onions	

Hanging baskets

These are great for plants such as tomatoes and strawberries that naturally 'trail' and hang. They will dry out quickly, though, as there isn't a lot of space for much soil in them, so you will need to water them even more than plants in pots.

Unusual and 'free' pots

Keep your eyes open around your home for other things you can use as containers for plants. Old crates, unused sinks, large tins and old colanders all make great containers. You could even try using some old Wellington boots!

Great plants for tiny spaces

Don't worry if you don't have a garden of your own. There are lots of plants that will grow happily in pots or other containers on a patio, balcony or even a windowsill.

Make the most of the space you have on your windowsill

Picking your pot

Always choose the biggest possible pot. Small amounts of compost dry out quickly, so plants in small pots need a lot more attention than those in larger ones. Above all, you have to be careful not to let the soil in any container dry out completely.

Pots as decorations

Try to choose different sorts of containers for indoor windowsills as they will be on show and it's good if they are prettier – and cleaner – than outdoor flowerpots!

Matching the compost

Try to match your choice of compost to the crops you want to grow. Most vegetables are happy with any multi-purpose compost, but acid-loving fruits such as blueberries prefer an 'ericaceous' compost. Longer-term crops such as apples and pears will need a soil-based compost, and you can replace the top layer of soil each year to refresh the nutrients. Peat-free composts are kinder to the environment.

You can put your containers in a place where it is easy to reach your crops and pick them to eat

Hanging baskets

These are great for growing cherry tomatoes, especially if you don't have much room. Hanging baskets will also keep your plants safe from slugs and snails, who like to nibble their leaves. Just make sure that the basket is not in the way – you don't want someone to hit their head – and remember to water your plants regularly.

Containers that used to be something else

Wellington boots
Old shoes
Wheelbarrows
Dustbin lids
Tin baths
Clean tin cans
Wooden crates

Kitchen colanders
Car tyres

*But make sure that no-one else wants to use them before you start planting!

Get growing

Get yourself kitted out

You can get started with just a few things. The tools sold for adults to use can be very heavy so, if you can, it's a great idea to get your own set in a size that's just right for you. Why not ask for a brightly coloured hand fork and trowel for your next birthday?

Pea sticks These are twiggy branches that are used to support plants such as peas.

Labels It's very easy to forget what you have planted. Write a label – old lolly sticks are perfect for this – and mark where you have put things as soon as you can.

Gloves Even if you love getting your hands dirty, you will need gloves for some jobs in the garden to stop your hands from getting scratched or stung by nettles.

Dibber A dibber is a piece of wood that is used to make small holes in the soil to drop in seeds or small plants into. A lolly stick, a pencil or even a plant stem can be used to do the same job.

keep a stock of labels so you can mark your planting as soon as it is done

Use tools that are the right size for you and try to get the best ones you can afford

Watering can

Seedlings and plants moved to new holes need watering. For seedlings, use a watering can with a rose attachment (added to the spout, this lets the water out in lots of tiny streams, which won't damage the seedlings). Take the rose off to puddle water around larger plants.

Spades Spades are used to dig holes, to dig up plants, to turn over the soil or to break it up. You can also use a spade to move compost around the garden.

Fork Forks are used for digging too, but they are more useful than spades for weedy ground, especially where there are lots of perennial weed roots that shouldn't be chopped up.

Hand trowel This is a mini spade that can be held easily in one hand. You can use a trowel to make small holes for small plants.

Hand fork A hand fork is a mini version of a full-sized fork. It fits easily in your hand and is used for digging around older plants.nts.

Rake A rake is the perfect tool for making sure your bed is free of stones.

Try to find a spade that is smaller than an adult-sized one. You can even get ones that have handles that you can make longer as you grow taller

Your hand trowel is your best friend. You can use it for all sorts of jobs in the garden

A hand fork is the same size as a hand trowel and just as useful, especially for levering out stubborn roots from pots

Your rake is especially useful in a new bed to make sure there are no stones or clumps of compost in the soil

You can manage without a hoe but they are extremely handy and can be used for all sorts of jobs, from weeding to helping you move soil when you are planting

If you can find one, a hand rake is a really good tool to own if you are growing things in a small space

mister You can only water really tiny seedlings with a very fine spray like the one from a mister. Otherwise, the little plants will be washed away.

seed trays Use these for sowing seeds. Fill a seed tray with compost and then sow your seeds onto the surface.

Pots You can sow big seeds such as sunflowers straight into pots.

sieve Use a garden sieve to get rid of lumps from compost when you are planting seeds.

string You use garden string to mark out lines to sow along and to support some kinds of climbing plants and to tie canes together to make a 'wig wam' to support things like beans.

25

Start seeds indoors while it's cold outside

While the soil is cold in spring you can start seeds in containers indoors. You can plant them in the ground outside when the weather warms up.

Seed tray or pot?

Small seeds need to be sown in seed trays and moved to pots when they have grown into small plants. Big seeds, like these bean seeds, should be planted straight into pots early in spring. They don't like cold soil so you have to keep them safe until the soil is warm enough to move the small plants into your veg plot. Fill the pots with 'seed compost': it is finer than multi-purpose compost and contains fewer nutrients, so the roots will grow large searching for food.

Gently fill the pots with fine seed compost

Reading the packet

Every seed needs different things. Some should be sown on the surface of the compost, some covered with a fine dusting of compost, others pushed below the surface. Always read the packet carefully!

Sowing from the palm

When you are sowing seeds, tip them out of the packet and onto your hand before sowing. If they are big, you should put only one or two on the surface of the compost in each pot. Try to put them into the middle, so that the seeds have the same amount of

Some of the tastiest foods — such as tomatoes and cucumbers — need to be sown indoors

room around each one. Then push each seed around 2cm into the soil and gently cover the hole with a little compost.

Watering after sowing

Once you have sown your seeds, they need water. A flood of water would churn up the soil, so use a watering can with a fine rose attachment, which will turn the gush of water into a sprinkle. Another way to water trays is to run a couple of inches of water into a sink or tray and leave the tray soaking for half an hour. After watering them, put the containers on a light windowsill or in a conservatory or greenhouse until they sprout (germinate).

Label the seeds and let them germinate on a light windowsill

27

Sowing Your seeds outside

From seeds to vegetables in one spot

Sowing seeds straight into the ground is much simpler than sowing them indoors. Lots of seeds are strong enough to sow outdoors (like lots of lettuces, carrots and beans) but some are not. Always check your seed packet before you plant.

Before You begin

Before you sow anything, make sure there are no weeds in your patch as they will fight your seedlings for light and water. Give your plants the best chance by providing them with a weed-free home where they can live without fighting for space.

Preparing the bed

Sowing your seeds in a straight line helps you to spot any weeds that invade your patch. Tie a piece of string to two sticks and then stretch it across your patch, pushing the sticks into the ground at each end. Following the line, use a trowel or a spade to make a long hole or trench in the soil (known as a 'drill') into which you can sow your seeds.

Use a piece of string tied on two sticks and pull it tight to mark a straight line

Sowing your seeds

Pour some seeds into your hand and pick a few up with the fingertips of your other hand. Sprinkle the seeds as evenly as you can along the drill, following the instructions on the packet for how many to sprinkle.

Settling in your seeds

Cover your seeds with a little soil, then water along the line using a rose attachment for a gentle rain of water. Write a label immediately as it is very easy to forget what you have planted.

Thinning the baby plants out

However thinly you sow your seeds, you will almost always need to take some of the weaker looking plants out later to make more room for the others. To do this, carefully take some of the seedlings out of your row so that the ones left have the same space on each side of them, and that space looks the same as the seed packet tells you it should be. Do this when the seedlings are small and water them straight afterwards.

the science

CHRIS EXPLAINS: THINNING OUT

Some seedlings such as carrots and lettuce benefit from a little competition after germination. When sowing, we use more seed than we need, and once the plants start to grow we thin out and remove the weaker seedlings, leaving only the strongest. This gives individual plants the space they require to produce big, healthy crops. Not all the thinnings go to waste – little bits of lettuce can go into a sandwich, but carrot seedlings should be put on the compost heap.

It may seem cruel, but you need to take out some baby plants to let the others grow

Looking after baby plants

As soon as seeds you have sown indoors have germinated (started to sprout), you will need to look after them carefully so that they produce strong leaves and roots and will be able to fend for themselves in the outside world.

Moving home

Moving a seedling from the crowded seed tray into its own pot is called 'pricking out'. You should do this as soon as the first leaves appear on the tiny plant. Hold the seedling by the leaf (never by the stem as it can easily be damaged). Gently push a dibber into the earth under the seedling and use it to help move the plant out of the compost from its roots. A lolly stick or a pencil will also work if you don't have a dibber.

seedlings need to be looked after carefully, especially when they are very young

the science

CHRIS EXPLAINS: BABY PLANTS
Some young plants like cucumbers and tomatos need extra protection from the cold. This is why their seeds are sown indoors. We describe these plants as 'tender'. Others are stronger and don't mind colder temperatures – we call them 'hardy'. Hardy plants like radishes or lettuces can be sown straight into the ground. Remember to read the seed packet to find out if your plants will be tender or hardy.

Preparing a new home for your plant

Fill a small pot with compost and tap it gently on the table top. This will help the compost settle. Use your dibber to push a hole big enough to hold your seedling's roots into the top of the compost, and then gently put the plant into the hole. We've used home-made newspaper pots for our young seedlings and you can find out exactly how to make these on pages 76-77.

If you don't have a dibber, use a plant stem, a twig or even a pencil

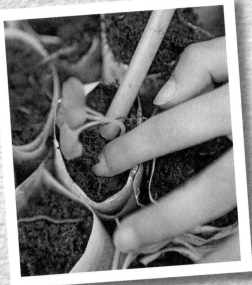

settling in

Use your fingertips to gently firm the compost down around the seedling, taking care around its delicate stem. Add a label to the pot straight away and then water your baby plant using a fine rose attachment. If you don't have one, ask an adult to make lots of little holes in the lid of a jar so that you can use this to sprinkle water on your plant.

It's tough out there ...

Plants can get a bit of a shock when they are moved outdoors as it's much colder. Getting your plants ready to be planted outside is called 'hardening off'. in late spring, when the weather is a bit warmer, put them outside for an hour or so on a warm day, then move them in when the sun goes down. Gradually increase the time your plants spend outside, always moving them back inside at night. After a week or so you can leave them out in a sheltered spot overnight for a few nights and, after this, they should be ready to live outside full time.

Watering wisely

Watering plants at the right time and in the right way stops waste and helps your plants to grow. Why not collect and use rainwater? Your plants will love it and you will be helping the planet too.

When to water

Always try to water your plants in the morning or evening as, in the middle of the day, when it is hot and sunny, lots of the water you add will evaporate before the plants' roots have time to absorb it. Some vegetable plants such as courgettes and lettuces can turn mouldy if you leave water sitting on their leaves overnight. Make sure you water these in the morning, so that the leaves are completely dry by evening. Basil is the one plant that should be watered in the middle of the day but never in the evening – it hates going to bed with wet feet.

Where to water

A clever way to be sure that plants in pots are getting only the water they need is to put them on a saucer and pour water into that, instead of onto the surface of the soil. The roots then absorb the water they need, leaving behind any they don't. An hour or so after you have added water, check the saucer and pour out any that is left over.

It's a good idea to add water to a saucer under your plants as then they will only use what they need

It is better to add a lot of water once a week to your veg plot than to add little dribbles of water every day

Saving water

You can buy special water butts to put in your garden to collect rainwater. Water is so precious that we should try to save as much as we can. If you don't have a water butt, remember that you can also recycle clean waste water from the kitchen on your plants – but remember that they won't like soapy or greasy water!

When have you watered enough?

When you are growing plants in pots, you need to know how much water they need so that you don't give them too little or too much. Remember that even if the soil on the surface of the pot is dry, there may still be plenty of moisture lower down. Poke your finger into the compost and if it feels damp you don't need to add more water. If it feels dry, you do.

How to weed and feed to grow superplants

Just like us, plants need plenty of food to help them to grow. Gardeners call these foods nutrients. You can find nutrients in soil, but they get used up easily, so we put them back by adding fertilisers. Plants also have to fight weeds for nutrients, water and light ... so get rid of them!

Two great ways to get rid of weeds

A hoe is a tool that is useful for clearing big patches of weeds. It slices off the tops of the weeds. Weed in between plants using a hand fork (a small fork that, as its name implies, sits in your hand), as you can be more careful not to cause any damage to the plants you want to keep. It's best to weed on a hot day as the sun will dry out any weeds you pull out and stop them from growing again.

Make sure that you dig out the whole root

the science

CHRIS EXPLAINS: ORGANIC FERTILISERS

There are lots of different fertilisers that all do different jobs. Liquid feeds are mixed with water. Some, like seaweed extract, are sprayed onto the leaves – they contain magnesium and iron, which are needed to make chlorophyll, a green pigment that helps plants to create nutrients. You can also add bone meal or chicken pellets directly to your soil – these will supply nutrients like nitrogen, which is important for leaves, and phosphorus, which is vital for roots.

Target the flowers

Some weeds spread using underground stems that you need to dig out, but many spread through their seeds. If you see a weed with flowers on, it is about to produce seeds that will grow into more weeds. So it makes sense to get rid of the weeds with flowers first.

Liquid goodness

Plants can be given a boost of nutrients, which can be added to your watering can. Mix it up, pour it on your plants and it will be taken in through their roots. Do this every few weeks in the growing season. Solid fertilisers work more slowly, but they feed plants over a long time. This sort of fertiliser is often included in compost mixes, but you can also buy plugs of them to push into the soil.

You need to measure liquid feed carefully. Don't be afraid to ask for help

Some liquid feeds can be sprayed directly onto the leaves

An extra boost for your pots

The soil in containers can get very low in nutrients. Potted plants need feeding every week, but you should also add a 'dressing' of a few handfuls of fresh compost to the top of your pots every spring. This is called top dressing.

Tasty, fresh food you have grown yourself

The best thing about growing your own food is eating it, especially if you started by planting seeds. Fruit and vegetables taste better when you have picked them yourself – they will be fresher than anything you can find in the shops and will have far more flavour.

Pick them only when they are ripe

When you buy fruit and vegetables from a shop, they may have been picked quite a long time before they were ripe. This is done so that crops can be carried to the shops wthout being damaged and so that they will store well, giving shopkeepers the longest possible time to sell them. But because they haven't ripened in the ground or on the plant, they are not likely to be nearly as tasty as when you can eat them just after you have picked them yourself. When you grow your own crops, you don't have to worry about how long it will take to get them to your kitchen and you can leave them to grow until they are absolutely at their best.

Harvesting from under the ground

Vegetables like beetroot and carrots (called root crops because you are actually eating their roots) can be picked when they are small and tender in the summer or left in the ground until winter. You can pick them from the same row at any time; you don't have to dig them all at once. In the summer, use a hand fork to help pull up the carrots you would like to eat. This will also make the plants less crowded, giving the ones that remain more room to grow. Eat the young carrots you take out and leave the rest until the autumn or winter.

Harvesting salad leaves

Salad leaves should be eaten as fresh as possible. Pick them carefully and your home-grown leaves will stay fresh until you are ready to eat them later the same day (try not to keep them overnight as they will go floppy and won't be nearly as good). Small salad leaves can be picked by cutting them at the base of each leaf with scissors. These small leaves will regrow, and are also known as cut-and-come-again leaves as you can go back to the same plant for more, time and time again.

Eat things immediately

Many vegetables start to become less tasty from the moment that you pick them, either because they start to lose their natural sugars or because they get tougher. Except for pears, which ripen off the tree, fruit should also be eaten as soon as possible.

Tasty, fresh peas —
sweet and delicious!

37

Brilliant plants that will get you growing

Here are some of the simplest and tastiest fruits, vegetables and herbs you can grow. If you don't know where to start, these pages will give you some ideas. And don't forget, you can always try growing other things once you've got the hang of growing these.

Mange tout

These crunchy green pods are eaten whole when they are young and sweet. They are great to grow as a vegetable-patch snack.

Winter squash and pumpkin

These fruits grow large over the summer and are picked in the autumn and winter to eat or carve for Halloween. When they are roasted, they taste sweet and nutty.

Potatoes

Home-grown potatoes taste so much better than any you can buy and it is really exciting finding the 'buried treasure' of waxy early potatoes under the ground.

Garlic

Pizzas and pasta sauces are twice as tasty when made with home-grown garlic.

Mange tout are tasty eaten straight from the plant

Garlic is very easy to grow

Potatoes you have grown yourself are like buried treasure

sweetcorn is great
fun to grow AND eat

perfectly ripe
cherry tomatoes

Cherry tomatoes

One of the stars of your vegetable and fruit garden! Nothing tastes quite as good as a fresh, ripe, home-grown tomato.

Cucumbers

Grow cucumbers that have small fruit, either in a greenhouse or outdoors, and you can enjoy sweet, crunchy cucumber all summer.

Carrots

Carrots are best picked and eaten in summer, when they are young. They grow well in deep pots if you don't have a vegetable patch.

Broad beans

Pick these when they are young and tender. Taking the beans out of their pods is fun too – the insides of their pods are furry.

Sweetcorn

Sweetcorn is really tasty when it is cooked and eaten just after it has been picked. It is delicious when you cook it on the barbecue.

Salad leaves

You can grow and eat different salad leaves almost all year round. They vary in flavour from mild lettuces to spicy oriental leaves.

Basil

Grow lots of basil and add handfuls of it to pasta or to put on top of pizzas. It is also tasty when added to salads with tomatoes.

Rosemary

Rosemary looks like a tough and woody herb but it has bags of flavour when you add it to food while it is cooking.

sunflowers grow quickly and will probably be the tallest flowers in your garden

Why not make your own strawberry cream tea?

Mint

If you like the taste of toothpaste or chewing gum, you will love mint. You can eat it fresh in salads, on potatoes or on top of berries!

Thyme

Thyme is used a lot in Italian food and pizzas and pasta wouldn't be the same without it.

Blueberries

Blueberries taste just as sweet and delicious straight off the bush as they do in muffins or cakes. The only bad thing is that they will only be ready to eat for two weeks every summer.

Strawberries

Try to let strawberries turn a glorious glossy red before popping them in your mouth. But it's hard to keep your hands off them.

Raspberries

Raspberries are easy to grow and will give you huge numbers of delicious summer and autumn fruits – gorgeous with ice cream.

Edible flowers

There are lots of flowers that can be eaten and others that definitely cannot. Check with a grown-up before eating any flowers, but marigolds, violas, nasturtiums and chive flowers can all be eaten and look lovely in salads or to decorate your plate.

Sunflowers

As well as for their huge, bright flowers, you should grow sunflowers for their seeds, which are really tasty after they have been roasted. And why not have a competition with a friend to find out whose sunflower grows the tallest or the fastest?

Projects to
grow your own

A windowbox full of herbs

A sunny windowbox is the perfect spot for growing herbs. But be careful that it is fixed safely to the windowsill as you don't want it to fall off and hit someone passing by!

1 PUT BITS OF BROKEN CLAY POTS OR SMALL STONES over the drainage holes in the base of your windowbox. These will add drainage and stop the compost washing out. Half fill the box with compost mixed with several handfuls of grit. Press it down lightly all over.

2 PUSH THE PLANTS OUT OF THEIR CONTAINERS FROM THE BASE and put them in the windowbox, trying out different arrangements until you like the way it looks. Trailing plants look good at either end, and more upright plants are best in the centre. Mint and basil should be planted in their own pots – mint grows strongly and may use too much space, while basil needs careful watering and it will be happiest growing on its own.

44

Keep your window-box in a sunny spot to give it the best light

3 ONCE YOU HAVE ARRANGED YOUR HERBS, use the same gritty compost to carefully fill in around the plants, firming down the soil with your fingers as you go. When you have finished, the compost should be a few centimetres below the top of the windowbox.

4 WATER YOUR PLANTS WELL and put the windowbox safely on a wide windowsill or support it with brackets. Make certain that it cannot fall off and hit anyone beneath the window. Make sure that you keep your windowbox watered.

Yum!

Tasty pasta sauce Add some basil leaves to the top of your tomato pasta sauce.

Sour cream and chive dip Snip chives into sour cream for a quick and tasty snack.

5 THE WONDERFUL THING ABOUT HERBS is that they love to be harvested. If you snip or pinch off the newest, freshest leaves or sprigs the plants grow even bushier. So harvest them regularly. Chives grow differently from other herbs, more like grass, and you should snip the leaves from the base with a pair of scissors.

45

A non-stop salad crop

'Cut-and-come-again' salad leaves are those that can be harvested several times from one sowing. You just cut what you need and the remaining plant grows back. Salad leaves grow quickly and are always fresher and tastier than anything you can buy at the supermarket. Why not try writing your name or initials in tasty little seedlings?

You can use a garden sieve to make sure your compost is free of stones and clumps

1 FILL A WINDOWBOX almost to the top with general-purpose compost. If you want to, you can use sand to mark out your name, initials or a pattern in the top of the compost where you are going to sow your seeds.

2 POUR SOME SEEDS INTO YOUR HAND and pinch small amounts of them between the fingers of your other hand. Scatter them along the marked-out lines of sand, cover them lightly with compost, then water.

3 WHEN THE SEEDS GERMINATE, thin the tiny plants out a little, taking a few away so that each plant is about 5cm from its neighbour. Eat these 'thinnings' as baby salad leaves.

cut your salad leaves regularly and they will grow straight back

4 TO HARVEST, use a pair of scissors to cut only what you want to eat in your next meal, popping it instantly into a plastic bag. Now wash your leaves. Fill the sink with cold water and add some ice cubes. Tip the leaves into the water and leave them for 10 or 20 minutes. They will fill with water and be crunchy.

Leaves all year round

If you choose the right plants, you can harvest salad leaves almost all year round. Winter salad plants are tough, but the leaves will be better quality and more tempting if you can grow them under cover. You can buy mini-polytunnels and cloches if you don't have a greenhouse.

Spring – pea shoots, baby spinach
Summer – basil and lots of varieties of lettuce
Autumn and winter (in a greenhouse, or under protective cloches) – oriental leaves, hardy lettuces

Tasty salads from seeds

You don't even need a windowsill to grow good things to eat – you can sprout seeds indoors and pick them at your table. Try growing some as 'micro leaves' that you can pick as tiny plants and eat others as just-sprouted seeds.

You will need a shallow tray and some kitchen towel

Growing cress and micro leaves

Sprouting seeds that you want to turn into green plants need plenty of light. Soak the seeds in water overnight, then scatter them thinly on damp kitchen towel in a shallow seed tray. You don't need compost. Put the tray on an inside windowsill and once your plants have rooted, make sure to keep the kitchen towel moist.

Before you sow some types of seeds you will need to soak them in water overnight

Scatter your seeds evenly by tapping the side of your hand

Not enough light?

You can grow sprouting seeds in jam jars or hessian bags as they don't need light. Soak the seeds in water overnight, then rinse and drain them. Put them in your jar or bag and rinse and drain them with fresh water every morning and evening for between three to eight days, depending on the variety. The seeds will swell up, so don't use too many. You can eat the sprouted seeds straightaway.

Time to pick

Some seed sprouts will be ready to pick after three days and others may need as long as ten. Pick the ones first that have grown the most and leave the others to grow a bit more. In this way you will get a few meals out of each batch. Rinse the seed sprouts well and eat them immediately, or store them in a plastic bag in the fridge for up to a week, rinsing them in clean water every few days.

Tiny micro leaves and sprouted seeds to try

Seeds that you can sprout in a jar: chick peas, barley, lentils, mung beans
Micro leaves that you can sprout on a tray: cress, wheatgrass, radish, alfalfa, buckwheat

How can I eat them?

Use sprouted seeds raw, either to add extra flavour to salad, or you can add them as a topping to a stir-fry.

sprouted seeds like beansprouts are deliciously crunchy

49

Growing perfect potatoes

Potatoes grow really well in a sack or another large container. Your potatoes will grow faster than they do in the ground and won't be attacked by slugs, so you will get the best possible result.

Start 'chitting' your potatoes in early spring

1 BUY SEED POTATOES from the garden centre. To give them the best start you can, make them sprout before you plant them. This is known as chitting. Put your potatoes in egg boxes or on a tray and leave them in a cool, light, frost-free place for a few weeks.

2 IN MID-SPRING YOU CAN PLANT YOUR POTATOES OUT. Fill the base of your container with about 20cm of compost (you can reuse old compost for this, if you want).

Early or late?

Potatoes taste quite different depending on whether they are picked early or late in the year. For new potatoes with soft skins that will need to be eaten immediately, harvest your potatoes after flowering has stopped. For larger potatoes with tougher skins wait until the leaves have yellowed and died down before picking. These are great to store.

3 PUT THREE SEED POTATOES ON TOP of the compost, evenly spaced, and cover them with another 10cm of compost. Water them well after you have planted them.

4 AS THEIR STEMS GROW UNDERGROUND, potatoes will grow along them. If they are exposed to the light they will turn green and become poisonous, so you need to keep covering them up with more compost. Do this at least once a week. Water them often and add a liquid feed once or twice a week.

Cover the stems with more soil as they grow

5 TO PICK YOUR POTATOES, tip the compost out of the container and dig around with your hands to find the potatoes. If you ask an adult to start boiling some water before you harvest your potatoes, you can eat them in as little as 15 minutes after they come out of the soil!

51

Grow tiny, sweet tomatoes in a hanging basket

'Tumbler' tomatoes grow perfectly in a hanging basket, their stems trailing down, covered with cherry-sized fruits. It's a brilliant way to grow tomatoes in a small space, but you have to be careful to water them.

You need a hanging basket, compost and one plant per basket

Plant some small flowers with your tomatoes to make your baskets colourful

1 LINE A HANGING BASKET, making sure there are holes in the base of your lining, and put a small circle of plastic cut from a strong bag over them. If the lining of your basket has no holes, ask an adult to use a screwdriver to make some to let water drain away.

2 FILL THE HANGING BASKET WITH MULTI-PURPOSE COMPOST. Run the compost through your fingers to make sure that there are no big lumps in the soil.

52

3 MAKE A HOLE IN THE COMPOST and plant the young tomato plant in it, pressing gently on the compost with your hands to make it firm. If you have more than one basket to fill, just use one plant in each. Why not plant flowers at the same time?

Plant lots of hanging baskets and you will have tomatoes all summer long

Press the compost down gently around your plants

4 TOMATOES NEED PLENTY OF FOOD AND WATER so water your baskets every day. When the flowers start to turn into fruits, feed with special tomato feed, which is high in potash, or liquid comfrey. Feed your tomatoes every week from now on.

Always water your baskets with a gentle sweep as the rush of water might be too much for your plants to cope with

5 IF YOU CHOOSE SPECIAL HANGING-BASKET TOMATOES YOU WON'T NEED TO DO THIS, but if you grow other types of tomatoes in the ground, in pots or growing bags, 'pinch out' the topshoots as they grow (this means that you should pull away the tiny new shoots) as this will make the plant bushy rather than too tall and will help fruit to grow.

special 'trailing' tomatoes grow well in a hanging basket but there's not much soil so you need to water them every day

the science

CHRIS EXPLAINS: PINCHING OUT SIDESHOOTS

You can stop your tomato plants from wasting energy growing too many stems by pulling off ('pinching out') little sideshoots, like in this picture. Flowers and then tomatoes will only grow on the stems that are left. By doing this, your plant will send all ithe nutrients it has absorbed to a smaller number of tomatoes, and they will grow bigger, stronger and even more tasty.

Yum!

Home-made tomato sauce Chop an onion into tiny pieces and fry it gently in some olive oil. Add your tomatoes and bash them with a spoon to break them up. Add black pepper and a few chilli flakes and, after 20 minutes, take the sauce from the heat. When it is cool, whizz it in a blender so that your sauce has no lumps. Although it's tasty cold, like home-made ketchup, you can also heat your sauce up and eat it with pasta. Yummy!

Tomato tart Put a frozen puff-pastry sheet on a baking tray, prick it all over with a fork, spread it with some tomato purée or your home-made tomato sauce. Put slices of your tomatoes all over the top and then add some of your home-grown herbs and some grated cheese. You could also add mushrooms or other vegetables. After 20 minutes in a medium-hot oven (200°C/400°F/gas mark 6), your tart should be ready to eat!

6 SMALL CHERRY TOMATOES ARE THE FIRST TO RIPEN. They will become sweeter the longer they are left to grow, so don't be too eager to eat them. Pick them only when they are perfectly red, and pop them into your mouth or into a salad.

Growing crunchy cucumbers

Cucumbers grow upwards *and* sideways. Make sure you choose a type that likes to be planted outdoors and give it plenty of room.

You will need a really big pot or ideally space in a raised bed, canes or old broom handles, string, cucumber plants

Save old broom handles and use these instead of canes

1 CUCUMBERS NEED lots of room. In late spring, find a sunny spot for your young plants in a raised bed or the biggest pot you can use. (Remember, if you have grown your young plants from seed, make sure they are big and strong enough before you think about planting them outside.)

2 USE CANES OR OLD BROOM HANDLES TO MAKE A SUPPORT for your plants to climb. Fill a large pot with compost and push three canes into it. (You can also do this in the ground.) Tie the canes with string at the top and then twice more further down, looping the string around the canes to create a kind of rope ladder. Plant one plant at the foot of each cane.

Plant cucumbers out in early summer then keep picking them — your plants will keep producing more fruits!

3 CUCUMBERS CONTAIN MASSES OF WATER – that's why they're so juicy. Give them lots of water every day when it's hot. They also like plenty of nutrients, so feed them once a week with tomato fertiliser or liquid comfrey.

Pick your cucumbers when they are small and sweet — perfect for your lunchbox!

4 TIE THE CUCUMBER STEMS into your cane and string 'wigwam' as they grow. Loop the string around the stem and then make another loop around the support – this will look like a number eight. The string 'eight' stops the cucmber from rubbing against the hard cane. Carefully harvest the fruits when they are still small, using scissors or secateurs.

57

Beans may need support!

Most beans climb high and need tall, strong supports. These are simple to make but can be a bit fiddly, so why not ask an adult to help you? It is best to sow your bean seeds indoors in pots to give them the greatest chance of success

1 FIRST YOU NEED TO MAKE A SUPPORT FOR YOUR BEANS. Make a long 'tent' from bamboo canes, tying them where they cross over at the top and adding a flat pole to the top as the picture on the opposite page shows. If you are sowing seeds straight in the ground, you should plant two seeds at the bottom of each cane and cover them with a protective cover called a cloche or with special horticultural fleece, as they are tender and need to be kept warm. If you have grown your seeds in pots, put one plant at the bottom of each cane.

the science

CHRIS EXPLAINS: 'SUCCESSIONAL' SOWING

If you sow a long row of seeds all at the same time, they will all mature at the same time too. 'Successional' sowing is a way of staggering harvesting time so that you get a small amount of perfect beans every few weeks instead of lots and lots of beans in the same week. It only works with plants such as French beans that crop quite quickly. Make a small early sowing of about six plants under cloches in mid-spring, and repeat every few weeks until late summer.

2 IT IS BETTER TO SOW YOUR BEAN SEEDS INDOORS IN POTS. Then you can let the seeds germinate in the warm and plant the baby seedlings outside in late spring, when the nights are warmer. These are French bean seeds.

58

If your beans start to grow in mad directions, you can wind them around the canes

3 YOUR BEANS WILL GROW UP THE CANES EASILY and may produce beautiful flowers, like the red runner bean flowers in the picture above. As they grow taller, you will need to gently tie the stems of your beans onto the canes.

4 WHEN YOUR BEANS ARE READY TO HARVEST, pick them frequently and they will keep producing more pods. You should pick pods from each plant every few days to prevent your beans from growing too big and too tough. Wash them and steam them so that you keep their fresh flavour.

Grow a monster pumpkin

Challenge your friends to a pumpkin-growing competition. One of the biggest so far is 821kg – do you think you can you beat that? Or, if you want to eat rather than compete, why not grow tasty winter squash to roast in autumn and winter.

the science

CHRIS EXPLAINS: REMOVING SIDE SHOOTS
When a pumpkin plant grows it sends out a couple of strong-growing stems and puts all its pumpkin-producing energy into them. After a while, smaller side shoots will start to appear and they will also try to produce pumpkins. To make sure that the main stems have lots of energy, you should take off these side shoots so that your plant will produce one or two really big fruits.

1 **PLANT YOUR PUMPKIN SEEDS** in pots and keep the seedlings well watered until they are ready to be planted outside. They are hungry and thirsty plants so when you do this, you will need to dig a big hole, about 30cm deep and wide and fill the bottom with well-rotted manure to give them extra nutrients.

Pumpkins love water so make sure you add plenty!

2 **USE A PROTECTIVE COVER CALLED A CLOCHE OVER YOUR SEEDLINGS. (You could use an upturned cut-in-half plastic bottle.)** Keep the seedlings well watered and feed them every week (or every few days if you want to grow a monster) with a liquid fertiliser.

3 IF YOU ARE TRYING TO GROW ONE REALLY BIG PUMPKIN, choose a single fruit that has grown early (it will have the longest possible time to grow) and take away all the other young fruits from the plant, putting them on your compost heap.

4 PICK PUMPKINS AND WINTER SQUASH in autumn in dry weather and before it gets too cold outside. They need a few days for their skins to 'cure' in the sun if you want them to store well. Leave them somewhere dry, ideally not on the ground. If it looks like it might rain, bring your pumpkins inside and keep them dry.

Cut your pumpkin open, scoop out the seeds, wash them and roast them for a tasty snack.

Grow the best corn

Grow sweetcorn plants in a block, either in a circle or two rows, to make a forest of plants that will grow from small seedlings to leafy plants nearly 2m high over the course of the summer.

Sow your corn on the cob seeds in late spring. Young plants can be planted in May

When your sweetcorn plants are small, wrap them up in horticultural fleece to protect them from the cold

1 **SWEETCORN CANNOT BE PLANTED OUTSIDE** until you are sure that the cold weather has passed, and they hate to sit in pots for too long, so don't sow them too early. Sow one seed per pot, indoors or in a greenhouse.

the science

CHRIS EXPLAINS: WIND POLLINATION

Many plants need to be pollinated before they can grow fruit. This means that pollen from the male flower has to make contact with the female flower. With some plants the pollen is carried by insects (particularly bees) or birds. Sometimes the wind carries the pollen into the air and hopefully onto the right part of the female flower. Sweetcorn is wind-pollinated, so if the plants are close together there is more chance of pollen landing in the right place and producing good, full cobs of corn.

2 YOUR SWEETCORN PLANTS will end up being really tall and, as you can see in the picture, once they have grown to the size of a ruler, they are strong and fast growing. Make sure you leave enough room between each plant for the leaves to spread out.

Yum!

Corn on the barbie Put a corn cob on a square of kitchen foil, spread the top of the cob with butter and sprinkle on some salt and pepper. Wrap the foil up and then ask an adult to cook the corn on the barbecue for you. It will need to be cooked for around 30 minutes and will need to be turned over every few minutes.

Corn on the cob Fill a big saucepan with enough water to cover your corn cobs, add a teaspoon of sugar and ask an adult to help you to boil the water and add the cobs. They will be cooked when they turn a darker colour of yellow. Take them carefully out of the water and cover them in lots of butter, add salt and pepper and then eat them messily ... but watch out, they will be very hot!

3 TO WORK OUT WHEN TO PICK YOUR CORN, watch out for when the tassles at the end of each cob begin to turn brown. If you think they might be ready, poke a fingernail into one of the yellow kernels and if a milky juice oozes out, your corn is ready to pick.

A stinky garlic garden

Lots of dishes, like pasta sauces, taste so much more exciting if you add garlic, and even better when you eat garlic bread with it too. And garlic is also really easy to grow!

You will need bulbs of garlic, grit for drainage, a hoe

Cover your gravel gently with a layer of soil. Use a hoe or a small fork to do this

1 FIRST USE SOME STRING to mark a straight line in your soil. Garlic needs well-drained soil, so dig a shallow trench and sprinkle in some grit.

2 PILE UP THE SOIL OVER THE GRIT making a mound like a mountain. Pat it down gently with your hands.

Plant garlic cloves in early spring and harvest in the summer

3 BREAK YOUR GARLIC BULBS UP just before planting. You can use garlic you have bought in the supermarket but it is always better to buy garlic from a garden centre as this will be free from diseases. Push the individual garlic segments (cloves) into the ground 10cm apart, until the tip of each clove is just below the surface of the soil.

4 GREEEN SHOOTS AND TALL LEAVES TELL YOU that your garlic is growing. (Make sure you water it well in dry weather.) You will be able to pick your garlic the summer after you planted it, as soon as these leaves start to turn yellow. Use a fork to dig under the bulbs and lever them up. Hang the garlic bulbs in an airy place to dry them out before storing them, or use them fresh for a milder taste.

Yum!

To make garlic bread, peel a few cloves of garlic, crush them with the back of a spoon and mix with soft butter and chopped parsley. Cut French bread into slices, but don't cut all the way through into the bottom crust. Add garlic butter to the slices. Wrap the loaf in kitchen foil and ask an adult to bake it for about 10 minutes, until the butter is melted. If you don't have much time, you can rub the top of buttered toast with peeled garlic for really quick garlic bread, like in the picture.

A strawberry fountain

Delicious, sweet strawberries grow well in pots. Fit lots of plants into a small space by stacking pots on top of each other, creating a tasty tower of berries.

Try out how many plants you need to fill your fountain before you start planting

1 CHOOSE A BIG POT AND A MEDIUM-SIZED POT. You are making a tower, with the smaller pot on top of the larger one. First fill the big one about three-quarters full with compost, then put the smaller one inside it and fill around it to the top. Then fill the smaller pot. Make sure that the smaller pot doesn't feel wobbly, and use your hands to firm down the compost in both pots.

2 BEFORE YOU PLANT THEM, WATER YOUR PLANTS WELL. When they have had a good soaking, you can start planting them in your tower. Put your plants well apart, and cover the tower completely. Water all the plants well.

Yum!

Eton Mess Break up some meringue nests into lumps and mix these with lots of whipped cream and some freshly sliced strawberries. Messy like its name, but delicious. And if you want to try something different, add some raspberries too.

Strawberry sandwiches This might sound funny, but freshly picked strawberries make really delicious sandwiches. Slice them thinly (ask an adult to help) and add a thick layer of berry slices to fresh white bread, thickly spread with unsalted butter. Sprinkle the fruit with crunchy sugar, add the other slice of bread and eat them as quickly as you can as they won't keep. If you feel like treating yourself, you could add a layer of whipped cream before adding the second slice of bread and if you feel adventurous, try adding a sprinkling of black pepper instead of the sugar. It really is good.

Plant your strawberries in autumn or early spring

3 FEED YOUR PLANTS EVERY TWO WEEKS with a high-potash feed such as liquid comfrey or tomato feed. This will help both flowers and then fruits to grow.

4 IN SUPERMARKETS, STRAWBERRIES OFTEN LOOK BEAUTIFUL but can be fairly tasteless. This may be because they have to be picked early, so they don't turn overripe and mushy on the journey from the farm to the shops. You should leave yours on the plants until they are deep red before you eat them.

Grow your own fruit salad

Choose a corner of your garden for fruit. You will probably have to stop the birds from eating your fruit as it grows, which is most easily done by spreading special nets over your plants.

Raspberries

Raspberries are very strong-growing plants so you will need to stop them from taking over your garden. Dig a trench as a barrier between your raspberries and the rest of the garden or they will also appear in the middle of your garden where you don't want them.

Some raspberry plants can grow very large so it is a good idea to give these extra support. The best kind of raspberries to plant are autumn raspberries as these need no support and you just have to cut the plants down to their base each winter to keep them strong.

Rhubarb

Rhubarb is really a vegetable, but gardeners treat it like a fruit so it deserves a place in your fruit garden. After planting rhubarb, water it while it gets settled in and then you will have to be patient. It takes two years for rhubarb stems to be ready to harvest. But NEVER eat the flowers because they are poisonous.

Blueberries

Blueberries like acid soil. If your soil is not acidic, or you are not sure, it is best to grow them in pots of ericaceous (acid) potting compost, which is perfect for them. Water the bushes with rainwater, if possible. Blueberries grow on neat little bushes and have beautiful glowing red leaves in autumn. Pick the fruits as soon as they ripen.

Raspberries are easy to grow and are fabulous with ice cream

Plant fruit bushes in late autumn or early spring, and rhubarb in spring

Blueberries are called 'superfoods' because they are so good for you. Tasty too!

the science

CHRIS EXPLAINS: ERICACEOUS COMPOST

Lots of plants like certain kinds of soil. Some plants, such as blueberries, are very fussy and like their soil to be acidic. But don't panic, if you want to grow blueberries and don't have the right soil in your garden, you can buy special compost called ericaceous compost from garden centres and use it to grow them.

Make a pizza herb garden

Pizza is simple to make – all you need is a base, a sauce and some toppings. Sauces for pizza are at their tastiest when they include fresh home-grown tomatoes and lots of herbs like oregano, basil and parsley. Make a pizza-shaped herb garden and fill each slice with a different herb. Add other tasty herbs like sage and rosemary and, when they have grown, you can get cooking and eating.

You will need a stick and some garden string, some stones or gravel to mark your circle, and plants

1 YOU CAN USE PIECE OF STRING TIED TO TWO STICKS to mark out a circle. Push one stick into the ground where you want the middle of your circle to be and then draw the circle with the other. Use more string to divide your plot into sections, like slices of pizza.

2 PLANT PARSLEY, OREGANO, GARLIC, SAGE, dwarf prostrate (growing low to the ground) rosemary, chives and rocket. Or you could just choose your favourites and plant up alternate 'slices', maybe using coloured gravel in between to separate them.

3 PICK HERBS AS YOU NEED THEM, but do try to do this regularly (or trim them) as it helps to keep the plants in good shape. Each time you remove the tender tips, you encourage side shoots to form lower down the plant, keeping it bushy.

Sow oregano and parsley in early spring or early autumn and basil all through spring

Yum!

To make a tasty pizza sauce using your herbs, start off by gently frying a chopped onion until it is soft and shiny, adding some chopped garlic towards the end. Pour on a tin of chopped tomatoes and let this bubble away for a few minutes until it thickens up. A pizza sauce shouldn't be watery. You can buy pizza bases or make your own. Spread your base with your sauce and then add your favourite pizza toppings together with loads of your home-grown herbs.

71

Giant smiley sunflowers

You can plant enormous sunflowers in your veg plot. Sunny
and happy-looking, they have seeds that attract the birds,
and you can roast the seeds and eat them yourself too.

Sow these huge
seeds indoors in
mid-spring, or
straight in the
ground outside
in late spring

1 SUNFLOWER SEEDS ARE QUITE BIG AND
SO ARE THEIR SEEDLINGS, so you only need
to sow one seed in each pot. Harden the little
plants off carefully, taking the pots outside
for short times when the weather is good, and
only plant your seedlings outside when the
weather is warmer.

2 SUNFLOWERS GROW REALLY TALL and
their flowerheads can be huge, so they will
probably need some extra support. Push a
cane into the ground next to the stem and tie
the plant's stem loosely to it. Feed frequently
with a liquid fertiliser to help it to grow.

3 YOU CAN MAKE A PATTERN, A SMILE, OR EVEN WRITE YOUR NAME IN THE FLOWER'S FACE by pulling out florets (the collections of little flowers that make up the single big flowerhead). As the flower grows, your picture will still be there.

Big, bold sunflowers feed the birds, and you too

4 WHEN THE PETALS START TO FALL OFF YOUR SUNFLOWER, SCRAPE THE SEEDS FROM ITS 'FACE'. You can roast them and eat them, or you could treat the birds – hang the entire flowerhead from the branches of a tree and they will love this nutritious winter food.

the science

CHRIS EXPLAINS: STAKING AND TYING

When we grow tall plants like sunflowers in pots or in our gardens, they may need some extra support to keep them standing up straight. Tomatoes, which often grow really tall but don't have strong woody stems, really like help to keep them upright – especially when they are young. You can use special bamboo canes, but broom handles or long sticks will work just as well. Make sure you tie the stems carefully, so that you do not damage the plants.

73

Keeping your crops tiptop

Fruit and vegetables often ripen all at once or so quickly that you can get tired of eating them every day. Store them properly or freeze them and you can enjoy them at another time.

Potatoes

When you harvest your main crop of potatoes, leave them in the sun for a few hours. Eat up any that are damaged or have holes in them where slugs could be hiding. Then brush off the soil and pack them into hessian bags. Take them all out once a month and check for soft or rotten ones, which you should throw away immediately.

Apples

Apples keep best in wooden slatted trays. They should be kept somewhere cool but away from frost and they need plenty of air. A shed is a good place, although you may have to throw some hessian or old blankets over them in really cold weather. Only store perfect apples and check them often. Throw away any that have gone mouldy.

Berries

Raspberries and blackberries can be frozen easily. Spread them out on a tray and put this into the freezer so that each berry freezes individually. When they have been frozen, you can then put them into bags or boxes. Doing it this way takes a little longer, but it prevents the berries from sticking together in a big lump and means you can take as many or as few as you need.

Make your own lollies

Making ice lollies is a great way of using up fruit, and you can store them for ages – but you will probably want to eat them quickly and make more. First mash your fruit to make it a thick liquid called a purée. Apples will need to be cooked with a little sugar to do this, but strawberries, raspberries and plums can just be whizzed up in a blender with a little water or fruit juice. Pour the purée into lolly moulds or ice-cube trays and freeze.

Mash up strawberries and freeze them to make smoothie lollies to share with your friends

How to make free pots for your plants

Start making paper pots in winter, ahead of seed-sowing time, so you will be ready when the busy season comes

You don't have to buy lots of pots for sowing seeds – you can make them out of old newspapers. And as well as being free, they rot away when planted in the ground, so they are also good for the planet.

You will need lots of old newspaper, a rolling pin and a mug it fits into snugly — or, like in the photos, a pot-making kit

1 BEFORE YOU CAN START, CUT A PILE OF STRIPS OF NEWSPAPER about 25cm long and 9cm wide. You don't need the pot maker shown above – you can use a wooden rolling pin and a mug into which it fits snugly.

2 ROLL THE PIECES OF NEWSPAPER AROUND THE ROLLING PIN OR POT MAKER, leaving a border of paper at the bottom. Tuck this up inside the newspaper tube.

Carefully fold in the bottom of the newspaper

3 AFTER YOU HAVE TUCKED IN THE NEWSPAPER BORDER put the paper tube into the cup and slide out the rolling pin. Make sure the newspaper covers the bottom of your pot. (Before doing this, you can use sticky tape to fasten the walls of your pot, but make sure you take it off before you plant them in the soil.)

4 FILL YOUR POTS WITH SOIL and stack them next to each other in a seed tray or shallow cardboard box. This will help them to stay upright. Sow large seeds such as beans directly into them, or use them for replanting ('pricking out') seedlings.

5 WHEN THE SEEDLINGS ARE BIG ENOUGH TO PLANT OUTDOORS, plant the pots straight into the ground. The roots will quickly push through the soft, wet newspaper, and the newspaper will gradually rot away. Magic ... and totally free!

Peas — treats you can eat straight from the plants

Peas really do taste best if you grow your own. This is because the sugar they contain starts to change to starch as soon as they are picked, so eating them straight from the plant is always going to be the best. You can eat them sneakily while you are gardening, fresh in salads or when they have been cooked very quickly in boiling water.

Watch out!

Mice love pea seeds and, if they get the chance, they will start nibbling them as soon as you've sown them. Keep your seeds safe by sowing them into a length of plastic roof guttering filled with compost. You can hang this out of the reach of the mice until the seeds have germinated ('sprouted').

1 PLANT OUT YOUR PEA SEEDLINGS when they are a few centimetres tall. If you have been growing them in guttering, dig out 'guttering-shaped' trenches in your soil and slide groups of the seedlings straight in, together with the potting compost. If you haven't used guttering, just plant them straight into the soil.

Sow pea seeds in the middle of either spring or autumn

2 PEA PLANTS LOVE TO CLIMB, so give them a climbing frame to scramble up. A row of sticks or twiggy prunings pushed firmly into the soil is perfect.

3 PEAS CAN BE TRAINED to grow up a wigwam of canes, either in soil or over a pot. Keep gently pushing their stems into the support and they will climb up.

4 THE MORE YOU PICK YOUR PEAS, the more pods your plants will produce. So keep eating the peas as soon as they are ready to pick – you can be a real pea pig!

Pop delicious, sweet little peas into your mouth straight from the plant

Six weeks until the big crunch

Growing carrots is super speedy. You can grow them in the ground, but they also grow really well in deep containers or raised beds, where they enjoy the loose, easily drained soil.

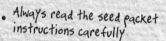
Always read the seed packet instructions carefully

Watch out!

Carrot flies smell carrots when they fly low over the ground. But you can be cleverer than them – if you grow carrots in a pot, you can keep the pots above the level at which carrot flies fly. They won't realise that they should make a detour. If your carrots are in the ground, put up a 60 cm 'fence' of plastic sheeting around them and the flies won't be able to get to your crop! You can also cover up the carroty smell by growing garlic, onions and herbs along your carrot row. Carrot flies also attack parsnips, parsley and celery.

1 TO PLANT CARROTS straight into the ground, make a long, shallow hole (called a seed drill) and sow your seeds along it. If you are growing your carrots in pots, scatter your seeds over the top and then sprinkle a light covering of compost over the top. Water the seeds and, if you are sowing them early in the year, cover the seeds with some horticultural fleece or a cover called a cloche to keep them warm and help them to germinate (sprout).

Sow in mid–spring or summer. Any you sow in summer will be ready to store for roasting in winter — yum!

Yum!

Little carrots are really sweet and are the perfect size to dip. Whizz up cream cheese, sour cream, garlic and some of your herbs, and use your baby carrots to eat it all up. Try using pieces of cucumber or little florets of broccoli and cauliflower too.

2 WHEN YOUR PLANTS START TO GROW, start taking out a few plants from the row to make extra room (thinning out). You can wash and eat the tiny carrots, if you like.

3 YOUNG RAW CARROTS ARE WONDERFULLY SWEET and crunchy, but any you leave in the ground will just keep on growing until you are ready to pull them up and cook them. It's a good idea to sow some carrots in the summer just so that you will have carrots to pick later in the season for storing into winter.

Carrots are ready for munching just six weeks after sowing — but big carrots like these will take longer!

Be a green gardener

Insect wildflower heaven

Because they are rich in nectar, a sugary liquid that bees and butterflies love, growing wildflowers is the best way to encourage insects to visit your garden. You don't need much room for a wildflower garden and lots of insects will visit and spread pollen from plant to plant.

1 BEFORE YOU BEGIN, MAKE SURE YOU GET RID of as many weeds as possible and use a rake to break up any big lumps of soil on the surface.

Getting ready

Your wildflower patch won't be exactly the same as anything you see in the countryside, but you can use your own mixture of flower seeds to grow a garden that looks very much like a country meadow. Try sowing some of these seeds, and you will like the results almost as much as the insects do:

Field poppy • cornflower • California poppy corn marigold • black-eyed Susan • larkspur love-in-a-mist • ox-eye daisy

2 SOW HANDFULS OF YOUR SEED MIXTURE in a zigzag. Then it will cover a large area and look natural.

Mix your choice of seeds together in a pot before sowing them in the ground

3 ONCE YOU HAVE SCATTERED YOUR SEEDS, use a rake to make sure they are lightly covered in soil. Water the patch well using a watering can with a rose attachment.

4 WHY NOT MAKE A SEED BOMB so that you can sow wildflower seeds in unloved patches of land? To do this, you will need to mix flower seeds and compost in a bucket with three times as much powdered clay. Add water until it is squelchy enough to squeeze the mixture into golf-ball sized balls. Leave these to dry and then, ideally in early autumn, throw them into your chosen patch of bare land. The autumn rain will soften your bombs and, with luck, flowers will grow in the spring.

A wildflower meadow is really beautiful, and insects will find it just as lovely as you will

85

Exploring a watery wildlife paradise

You don't need a pond to add water to your garden. You can bury a bucket or an old dustbin lid in the ground and fill it with water. Don't forget that adding water to your garden may bring frogs and toads and these will also eat slugs, the number one veg-patch enemy!

Pond dipping

If you do have a pond, take some water out of it with a bucket. Then wave a fishing net in the water. If you find any mini-beasts in the net, empty them into the bucket for a closer look. Or you may find some wobbly frogspawn jelly.

Fantastic frogspawn

Don't worry, if you don't have your own pond, you can still hatch tadpoles. In the spring collect a jar of frogspawn from a local pond and put it in a bucket or fish tank. It is probably too hard to look after them all the way from blobs of jelly to frogs without a pond, so hatch them, then return them to the pond where you collected them.

Ponds can be dangerous! Take care when exploring them and make sure the water is always shallow.

Planting for ponds

Plants are really important to ponds. They make shady spaces on the pond edges – these give shelter to wildlife and help to keep the pond water cool. Some plants even grow under the water and add oxygen to the water, which is good for pond animals.

Help wildlife to thrive

A wildlife pond needs sloping edges so that animals can crawl in and out easily. Other animals can use the edges to stand and drink fresh water from the pond without falling in. A gravel slope is perfect.

Home, sweet home for your birds

Birds can sometimes be a nuisance in your garden by eating berries. But they also eat pests so you should welcome them into your garden – just be careful to protect any fruit ripening in your plot.

Birds need water too

Birds need water all year round. Put a bird bath somewhere where there are no cats nearby. But make sure it is also fairly close to a bush or tree where they can escape to if they sense danger. Keep the bath topped up, especially on hot summer days, or in the winter, when it's really cold and you may need to break the ice.

the science

**CHRIS EXPLAINS:
THE IMPORTANCE OF BIRDS**
Birds are really important in the garden because they kill pests like slugs and other creatures that will want to eat your vegetables. There are lots of ways to get birds to visit the garden but making sure there is water in your garden is a very good way to bring them in. Birds are very clean creatures and need to look after their feathers, so you can enjoy watching them wash in the bird bath.

Give birds a place to hide and shelter so they will feel safe and keep visiting your garden

Lots of shelter

Birds need lots of different places to shelter around the garden. They particularly love thick hedges, which serve as a place where they can live safe from predators. Hedges are also a 'wildlife corridor', making bridges from one wildlife-friendly place to another. If you have plenty of space and trees, hang roosting boxes in trees and bushes – birds can shelter there during the day and they may return in the spring to nest in them.

Keeping crops safe from birds

Growing fruit in a fruit cage (a huge frame covered with a net) is the best way to keep birds away. If you can't do this, keep some netting ready to cover fruits like cherries and raspberries as they start to ripen. Make sure that you stretch the net as tightly as possible and fix it firmly – if the net flaps about, birds can get caught in it. But take the net away each time you pick your fruit and then take it off completely when the whole crop has been picked – then the birds can come in and eat any pests left behind.

Great homes for birds

Put up a nesting box in your garden because, if you are lucky, baby birds will be born there. It's more difficult to do this if you live in a flat so why not share a bird house with a friend who has a garden?

What box should I choose?

If you live in a town, choose a small box because garden birds like blue tits and sparrows like them better than a larger box. If you live in the country, put up a larger box for woodpeckers, thrushes or even little owls. Special boxes with an open front are perfect for robins.

What should my box be made of?

Wood is great for bird boxes as is 'woodcrete', which is a mixture of wood and concrete. Try to make sure that the wood is long-lasting hardwood. Bird boxes should have holes in the base to let things drain away and holes in the top to let in the air.

Why not ask for a nesting box for your next birthday?

Decorate a bird house with your favourite colours and stickers

Where should I put it?

Ask an adult to help you to fix your box on a tree, wall or post between 2 and 4m from the ground. Chose a spot where the entrance is sheltered from wind, rain and strong sunlight. Tilt the box forwards a little so that rain won't fall into the entrance. Make sure birds can fly easily to and from your box. Open-fronted nest boxes should be fixed about 2m from the ground and their entrances should be hidden by trees, bushes or branches.

How do I look after for it?

Birds will be less likely to come back to your box if it is filled with last year's twigs and leaves. You should clear all this rubbish out between late summer and mid-winter. Before you do this, watch the box for a few days to be sure no birds are using it, then open it up. Put any rubbish into a plastic bag and put this into the bin. Wash the box out with hot water (but don't use soap or washing-up liquid) and leave it to dry.

I wonder which bird box the birds will like best?

91

A bird-feeder buffet

Mixing bird seed with fat will give the birds extra nutrients that they can store for the cold winter months. It also binds the seeds together so it can be made into cakes to hang up.

You will need half a coconut shell, suet (fat), wild birdseed mix, string

1 ASK AN ADULT TO HELP YOU TO MELT A BLOCK OF SUET (a kind of fat) in a saucepan and then add just enough wild bird food to give every seed a generous coating of fat. Give it a good stir because dry bits will not stick together. Suet can be made of animal or vegetable fat – use whichever you want.

2 ASK AN ADULT TO MAKE A HOLE IN THE bottom half of a coconut shell or an old yoghurt pot. (Do NOT try to cut the coconut yourself as it is VERY hard.) Thread a piece of string with a knot tied in one end through the hole.

3 SPOON THE FATTY SEEDY MIXTURE IN, pressing it down firmly. It won't look tasty to you but the birds will love it. Leave to set.

4 ONCE THE FATTY MIXTURE HAS SET, hang your coconut or yoghurt pot from a high spot, like the branch of a tree. It should be too difficult for cats to reach. Choose a shady spot, as the suet will melt if it gets too warm. You could also hang strings of peanuts and rings of apple for the birds. You will now be able to watch birds visit, knowing that they are filling themselves up with fats to help them through the cold winter nights.

Don't forget to keep your bird feeders topped up with wild birdseed mix too — birds need lots of help

93

Bees need homes too

Bees, like lots of insects, are very good friends to gardeners. In the winter, they like to crawl into small spaces to keep safe and warm. You can make them the perfect winter home using bits and pieces.

1 ASK AN ADULT TO CUT A BUNCH OF HOLLOW-STEMMED BAMBOO CANES to about the same length as a ruler. Using garden string, tie them together tightly at each end.

2 MAKE A HANDLE for your insect house by tying another piece of string between the other strings, leaving a long loop so you can hang it from the branch of a tree.

Bees like to nest in small spaces, but all sorts of other insects will visit your insect house as long it has spaces of different sizes

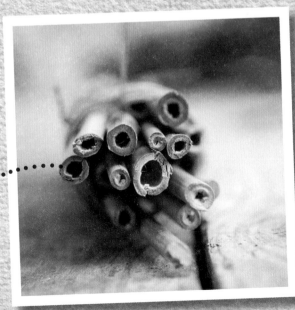

3 MAKE A WILDLIFE HOTEL AS WELL. Find an old bookcase or ask an adult to make some shelves out of pieces of plywood, and then put dividers in to make a series of small boxes. Fill these with stick bundles, bricks with holes in them, old pieces of wood, bundles of straw and twigs, and whatever else you find that you think might make a good home for an insect.

4 IF YOU DON'T HAVE ANY BAMBOO YOU CAN USE TWIGS to make your insect house or hotel. Tie twigs of the same length together and find a dry, cosy place to push them into, perhaps into or under a hedge, or along the side of a shed. The insects will soon move in.

Going batty

Gardens with lots of insects are often visited by bats and it's very exciting to see them swooping around on summer evenings. To encourage them into your garden, try to plant lots of flowers that smell good. These will attract the insects that bats eat. You should also make plenty of winter homes for insects as then there will always be food for any bats that are visiting. You could also build a bat box, which is a bit like a bird box but doesn't have a bottom. A pond or some other water nearby will also help them to make a home in your garden. You could just sink an old bucket into the ground and fill it with water – but be careful that it is somewhere safe where nobody can fall into it or step into it by mistake.

Worms can make plant food

You can use bits of leftover food from your kitchen to make compost and liquid feed. If you add a handful of tiger worms to your wormery, they will eat up your scraps and, in return, they will even turn them into compost and liquid feed for you.

Wormeries are great fun. There are two sorts. Some have a series of trays through which the worms move as they eat the waste and make compost in return. It is easy to take the compost out of this sort of wormery – you just wait until all the worms have moved into the next tray, then lift it out. Others are more like a large bin from which you can take free compost every six months or so.

Your wriggly worms

When you buy a wormery, it comes with a pack of special worms. Put them in the wormery with some shredded newspaper for their bedding and a handful of veg scraps from the kitchen, chopped up small.

The wriggly worms move from layer to layer, leaving great things behind

It takes the worms a while to settle into their new home, but once they start eating at full speed, you should be able to put most of the scraps from your kitchen into your wormery. Every now and again, you will need to sprinkle the worm compost with some calcified seaweed, which probably came with your wormery. Adding this will keep the compost just as the worms like it. You can also add crushed eggshells.

Using your juice

Use the wormery's special tap to drain away the liquid feed that the worms make, or else the compost the worms also make may be too wet. Add water to this liquid to make a fantastic free feed to use on all your plants.

They don't just sting you

Another way of producing your own fertiliser is to crush some nettle or comfrey plants (wear strong gloves while you're doing this) and leave them to soak in a bucket of water for three or four weeks. The bucket will get very smelly, so put it well away from the house. When it has stewed, mix a small amount of the smelly liquid with ten times as much water as you have smelly liquid. Pour this into a hand mister, and on a still day, spray this mixture (which will be really rich in nitrogen) onto the leaves of your plants.

New plants for nothing

You don't have to buy new plants – just learn how to grow new ones from the ones you have already. Taking cuttings, collecting seeds and dividing up your plants are easy ways to grow more ... for free!

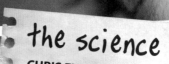

Make new plants in autumn and spring by splitting plants into more than one or growing new ones from cuttings

Collecting seeds

You can gather seeds easily from French, runner and broad beans, peas, chillies and lettuce plants. To grow seeds to plant for next year's crops, first you will need to choose the plant from which you are going to collect seeds. Then don't pick anything from that plant as it grows, however tempting it might be. When the plant's crop is finished, choose a dry day to harvest your seeds. Pick off the seed pods, pop them, pick out the seeds and store them in a dry air-tight container in a dark place away from the sun. Then you will be able to grow plants for nothing!

Store collected seeds in an airtight container in a cool, dark spot, and sow them the following year

the science

CHRIS EXPLAINS: GROWING NEW PLANTS FROM CUTTINGS

Seeds can remain dormant (not starting to grow) until they are happy with the conditions around them. In spring, when the days start to get longer and warmer, it's a good time for them to grow. This also makes spring a good time to take cuttings. Plants contain a group of cells known as the cambium, which helps them to grow roots. As the plants start to grow in spring, the cambium cells begin to work and there is a greater chance that your cutting will produce roots.

Making baby plants

If you want lots of herbs, take cuttings from the ones you already have. Grow sage, rosemary, thyme and lemon verbena from cuttings you take in the spring. Cut a stem about 10cm long, with no flowers on it. Take off any leaves from the bottom third of the stem and push it into a pot of compost, right up to the leaves. Water, cover the pot with a clear plastic bag and put it on the windowsill. You will know the cutting has rooted when new leaves start to appear.

Before you buy new plants, learn how to grow more from the ones you own already

Splitting up your plants

Some plants can be divided (split up) in autumn – herbs like mint and thyme, for example. Ask an adult to help you to lift the whole plant from the ground and then, between you, use a spade and your weight to split it in half. If the plant is really big, you may want to split it up again, into four or even smaller pieces. Replant all the plants straight away and give them lots of water.

Growing from 'runners'

Strawberries grow 'runners', which are long stems that root where they land and make new plants. It is easy to dig these up and put them in pots. You can give these away to friends but you will need to start again from new plants every three years.

What's gone wrong?

Here are a few of the problems that you can have with your crops.
But if you are ready for them, you won't have many disasters.

Slugs and snails

These little terrors cause the most problems in vegetable gardens. They can eat a whole row of seedlings in one night and can cause huge amounts of damage to young plants. You need to turn to page 106 for ideas on how to deal with them because you really can't let them beat you!

Snails might be fun to watch as they slither along, but they will eat your young plants

Sap suckers

Aphids are pests that swarm over the soft parts of plants and suck out their sap (the liquid that moves food and water around your plants). Pests like whitefly, greenfly and blackfly stop plants from growing well. Look on page 104 for ways to encourage insects that eat aphids to eat your pests.

Know your enemies and you will win your battles against them

Wiggly caterpillars

Caterpillars nibble holes in leaves. On most plants this isn't a big problem, but some caterpillars can take all the leaves from a plant very fast. Some plants like cabbages are particular favourites of caterpillars.

Not enough water?

If you don't water your seedlings enough after you have planted them, they will look sad and floppy. Make sure you give them lots to drink every day until their roots have grown big enough to find water in the soil themselves.

Your vegetables will be small and less tasty if you do not remember to water them regularly

Danger from the skies

Birds can pull up onions, shred and eat brassicas (another name for members of the cabbage family), eat ripe berries and even seeds before they have germinated. Put nets over your fruit bushes and cabbages as soon as you plant them outside. Try making a scarecrow to keep birds away from your seeds. You will find more ideas on page 108.

103

Your plants' best friends

Some plants get along with each other better than others. 'Companion planting' is when one plant really helps the one that it is planted next to. Perhaps the smell of one hides the smell of the other and keeps pests away, or maybe one plant attracts pests and keeps them off the one you are growing to eat. By helping each other, these plants are 'good companions.' Here are some ideas.

Beans and nasturtiums – aphids like eating beans, but they love nasturtiums even more. The nasturtiums act as 'trap' or 'decoy' plants, luring the aphids away from your crop.

Carrots and onions – carrot flies find their favourite food (carrots!) by smelling them, but the smell of onions confuses the flies and makes it harder for them to find the carrots.

Cabbages and dill – hoverflies and other insects that eat aphids really like dill so, with dill on offer, they will leave your cabbages alone. Dill is also a great herb to eat, especially with fish.

Tomatoes and French marigolds – aphids are said to hate the smell of French marigolds so they keep away.

Fruit trees and poached-egg plants – Poached-egg plants attract lots of good insects, some of which will find their way on to your fruit trees and spread pollen between them, encouraging them to grow fruit.

Ladybirds can protect your plants by munching on aphids and other garden insects

Sweetcorn, beans and winter squash – the squash shades the roots of the other plants and stops them from losing moisture, while the sweetcorn provides a 'pole' for the beans to grow up. They grow very well together and are known as the 'three sisters'.

Tomatoes and basil – some gardeners say that growing basil with tomatoes makes them taste better.

Basil and tomatoes taste delicious together, so why not grow them together too?

Aphids think that the smell of French marigolds is horrible, so if you grow them near tomatoes the aphids will stay away from both plants.

Smelly onions will confuse pesky carrotflies from finding and destroying your carrot crop

The great vegetable destroyers

Your main enemies in the veg plot are slugs and snails. But don't panic, there are lots of weapons that you can use against them.

Slugs and snails love young, soft plants and can eat a whole row of seedlings or baby plants overnight. Although you might see them during the day, they are at their most dangerous at night, when it is cooler and damper and they find it easier to move around and munch. Although barriers and slug hotels work, slug pellets are the best way to keep slugs away. But they can be poisonous so choose pellets that contain a chemical called aluminium sulphate as these are the least likely to harm other animals. Be very careful with slug pellets as they can poison you too so always ask an adult to help you with them.

The slug Hotel

Make a slug hotel (a trap for slugs) by burying a jam jar or plastic container in the ground just up to the top of the container. Fill it with beer and the slugs will come slithering in, following the smell of the beer. Once they have visited, they won't be allowed to leave as they will drown in the beer – so empty them away each morning.

the science

CHRIS EXPLAINS: SLUG BARRIERS

If you turn a slug or snail upside down you'll find a large area called a foot underneath it. This foot is what enables these creatures to get around, but in order to work properly it needs a smooth, damp surface. Putting down barriers of something dry and rough like gravel makes it more difficult for the slug or snail to move. Make a ring of sharp grit around your plants – this will help keep slugs away.

Ask an adult to give you some beer for your slug hotel. Any will do, but slugs really like lager

106

A line of gravel or grit will help keep the slugs and snails away — but make sure there are no gaps in your barrier (or the slugs will find them) and also add some slug pellets to your gravel. But be careful!

You can even crush up old egg shells and use these to make a sharp and pointy slug 'wall'. Like the gravel barrier, it's a good idea to mix in some slug pellets — but remember they can be poisonous to you too

107

(Not so) scary scarecrows!

Scarecrows are great fun to make but even the best ones don't seem to scare the birds away for long. Make your own scarecrow, using old clothes – choose a funny combination as your scarecrow can look as strange as you like.

1 FIND TWO PIECES OF WOOD – one about half as long as the other – and ask an adult to nail them together to make a cross. Old broom sticks work well. The shorter piece will be the arms of the scarecrow, and the longer one will go into the ground.

2 STUFF A PAIR OF OLD TROUSERS with straw or another stuffing material, like scrunched-up newspapers or other old clothes. Tie string around the trouser bottoms to hold in the stuffing. Put a shirt onto the 'arms' of the cross and then ask an adult to roughly sew the trousers to the bottom of the shirt, or you can use old braces to hang the trousers from the scarecrow's arms. Stuff the shirt with straw and tie the cuffs together with string so that the stuffing stays in the shirt, too.

3 NOW MAKE A HEAD. This can be an old football, a pumpkin, an upturned bucket, or anything round and light. You can even sew your own head from an old pillowcase that you can stuff. Don't put its head on yet.

4 WHEN YOU HAVE FINISHED YOUR SCARECROW choose its spot in the garden and ask an adult to use a mallet to bang it deep into the ground. Now you can add your scarecrow's head to the top of the pole and even add an old hat or scarf if you have one.

A scarecrow may not keep birds away from your plants for long but it will look great anyway!

Other scary things!

While scarecrows look great and are a lot of fun to make, birds can get used to them and stop being scared by them. Scarers that make a noise or flash in the sunlight work much better and will keep birds away for longer, even though they will get used to these too.

Twirly windmills

Jazzy windmills are great for scaring birds away for short times. Tie them onto your fence or plant them in a flower pot. Even when there's only a little bit of wind, they will spin around and their colours will flash in the sunshine, keeping the birds away.

Flashing lights

Hang strings of shiny beads in the sunshine and they will sparkle in the light as they move in the wind. Old CDs are also perfect for this and already have a hole in the middle which you can loop string through.

Birds can get used to scarers really quickly. Use brightly coloured windmills like these only for as long as you really need them — like when your berries are ripening. Next time, try something else!

110

Noisy scarers

You can make a bell-chime scarer like this one with a piece of wood, string and old bells of various sizes. You can buy bells in craft shops or take them from unused cat or dog collars. Cut a long bit of string and tie it to each end of the wood. Cut a piece of string for each bell and tie them onto the twig in a row. Make sure you leave just enough space between the bells so that they touch each other when the wind blows and make a jangling, tinkling sound.

If you don't like the sound of bells, collect shells, beads and bits of wood and tie a piece of string around each. If you need to make holes in anything, ask an adult to help you. Tie your collection of things to pieces of string, and wrap them, round an old coathanger, making sure that the strings are close enough for the shells and beads to knock together

Index

Acknowledgements

All photographs are by Will Heap for Octopus Publishing, apart from the following:

Bigstock sdenness 40 right, 63 below

Fotolia awfoto 95 above left; benamalice 73 above; ChristopheB 100-1; Denis Nata 63 centre; Edyta Pawlowska 68; fdoimages 71 below; merryll 65 above right

GAP Photos Dave Bevan 105 below; David Dixon 54 below; Fiona Lea/design Sue Beesley 87 above; Friedrich Strauss 72 right; Graham Strong 105 above; Martin Hughes-Jones 62; Mel Watson 67 left; Paul Debois 18 left; Zara Napier 79 above right, 103 below

Getty Images D Normark/PhotoLink 63 above; Sudo Takeshi 98 below

Octopus Publishing Group Anton de Beer18 right, 70 left & right, 71 above, 90 above, 108-111; Freia Turland 19 left, 102 above & below

Thinkstock Comstock 32 above; Hemera 1, 5 below, 30 above, 36, 37 above & below, 75 above, 78 right, 88 above, 95 below, 96 right, 103 above; iStockphoto 8-9, 31 below, 37 centre, 38 left, 59 all, 60 above & below, 74 left, 78 left, 79 above left, below left & right, 90 below, 107 above; Jupiterimages 30 below, 42-3, 61 above & below; Martin Poole 49 above; Medioimages/Photodisc 41 right, 73 below

Daisy, windmill, notepaper and tag used throughout: Fotolia/ecco; Fotolia/barneyboogles; Thinkstock/iStockphoto; Thinkstock/Hemera

The publishers would like to thank the following:

Will Heap for the beautiful photographs, and for bringing along his whole family to take part

Mary Caroe for all her hospitality and generosity in allowing us to photograph in her beautiful gardens: www.vanngarden.co.uk

Emily Caroe for allowing us access to her garden, and for making us so welcome

Our models: Isobel Brooks; Anastasia and Joseph Glass; Carla, Ashleigh and Emily Rochester; Hugo Brown; Emily and Daniel Scartlebury; Mary, Calum and Penny Skuodas; Tom, Scarlet and Stanley Heap; Mia and Scarlett Somerville; Reece Merritt

Boden for loaning us the gorgeous children's clothes: www.boden.co.uk

Crocus for the loan of the fantastic children's garden tools, the birdbath and waterfall watering can:www.crocus.co.uk